# Story Fest

# Story Fest

## Crafting Story Theater Scripts

Dianne de las Casas

Illustrated by Jeanne de la Houssaye

Teacher Ideas Press, an imprint of Libraries Unlimited
Westport, Connecticut · London

British Library Cataloguing in Publication Data is available.

Library of Congress Catalog Card Number:
ISBN: 1-59469-009-X

First published in 2006

Libraries Unlimited/Teacher Ideas Press, 88 Post Road West,
Westport, CT 06881
A Member of the Greenwood Publishing Group, Inc.
www.lu.com

Printed in the United States of America

The paper used in this book complies with the
Permanent Paper Standard issued by the National
Information Standards Organization  (Z39.48–1984).

10   9   8   7   6   5   4   3   2   1

*For Bissonet Plaza Elementary*

*Especially Extraordinary Ellen Miller*

Dianne de las Casas

*For Joyce Kelly*

*She was my hero*

Jeanne de la Houssaye

# Contents

# Introduction

As a professional storyteller, I perform and present artist residencies in schools. In my residencies, I work for an extended period with the students, teaching them storytelling techniques. The residency often culminates in a student performance of "The Story Fest." Much of my residency work focuses on Story Theater.

While I thoroughly enjoy working with the students and teachers in the classroom, my ultimate goal is to empower teachers by providing them with the coaching skills and tools for them to be able to continue the work I have begun. That is the basis for this book. Story Theater is a fun process for both the Story Coach and the students, allowing everyone to bond through group work, problem solving, and the joy of sharing a well-told story.

My goal was to create scripts that allowed whole class participation in the story. The *Story Fest* tales are designed for use with a classroom-size group of students. Students who enjoy the limelight can take on the role of the storyteller while those who prefer a supporting cast role can choose to be in the chorus.

I also hope that you will try your hand at crafting your own story theater scripts. There is a rich world of folklore, myths, and legends waiting to be brought to life through a storyteller's pen and tongue. Here's to celebrating a festival of stories!

# The Story Theater Process

## Introduction to Story Theater

According to The New College Edition of *The American Heritage Dictionary*, the definition of "story" is "the narrating or relating of an event or series of events; either true or fictitious." The definition of "theater" is "dramatic literature or performance." By combining the two, Story Theater comes to mean "the narration of events through dramatic performance."

In traditional theater, there is a "fourth wall," where actors only interact with each other. Unlike traditional theater, Story Theater has no "fourth wall." The storytellers interact directly with their audience. In Story Theater, the storyteller performs or dramatizes the stories with great flair through vocal inflections, facial expressions, and body movement.

For the teacher on a limited budget, Story Theater is a great way to involve the entire classroom in a full production without having to spend a lot of money on costumes and props. Simple props and costumes can enhance the presentation of the stories and ideas for those will be given later. The stories are strong enough to stand on their own through the power of the storytellers, eliminating the need for expensive play fees.

Another important element to remember is that there is no one right way to tell a story. Every storytelling style has value. With that in mind, storytelling and Story Theater is a perfect way for students with varied learning styles to communicate their creativity.

## Establishing an Environment of Trust

To "break the ice" so that the students can get to know me better, I always tell them a story about myself, often a story about an experience I had at their age. This helps to bridge the gap and allows them to get to know me better, thus allowing them to trust me. If your students already know quite a bit about you, try inserting a new personal story or share an experience and ask for their feedback. Perhaps find an experience to share that will introduce the story theater activities you will be using.

In theater, trust is very important. Actors often expose themselves and their emotions in a way never seen before. It is the same for the students. Some of the students may have never had the opportunity to role play or act out a part and may feel uncomfortable doing so in front of their peers. For example, a boy might play the part of an old woman. To establish the environment of trust, I introduce "The Classroom Contract," a contract for grades three and up that enforces respect and prevents teasing.

It is read orally and at the end of each statement, the students say, "I agree." It helps set expectations and guidelines for the duration of my work with the students.

### Classroom Contract

The Number One Rule is RESPECT:

RESPECT FELLOW CLASSMATES - I will respect my classmates at all times. I will not laugh at them, make fun of them, or make them feel bad.

RESPECT TEACHER - I will respect [Teacher's Name] by listening to her [him] and following directions. Failure to do so will result in a behavior report [or other means of discipline suited to your school's environment].

RESPECT OTHER PEOPLE'S PROPERTY - I will respect other people's property including things that belong to my fellow classmates and my teacher(s). I will take good care of borrowed items and put them back where they belong.

Although I find that an oral contract suffices, you can provide a signature line and have each student sign the contract. If the class becomes unruly, I simply pull out The Classroom Contract and issue a gentle reminder.

# Preparing for Group Work

When beginning activities for story theater work, I start with individual exercises and lead into partner exercises. I culminate with group work. This helps to ease the students into their roles, allowing them to get a feel for the material and establish a comfort zone.

I often ask students to explore roles they would not normally take. For boys, this may mean playing the role of a female. For girls, this may mean playing the role of an animal. It varies with the students and the class. I like to pair co-ed partners. With third grade and up, I explain that they will be choosing a co-ed partner, a partner who is a member of the opposite gender. I explain, "That means boys will choose girls and girls will choose boys." If this request is met with reluctance, I explain, "As we travel through life, we are expected to work with all types of people. It's good to get some practice now." After the first exercise, co-ed partnerships are no longer an issue.

Once I move through the partner exercises, I move into some group exercises, either dividing the class into small groups of 4-5 or by dividing the class into two groups. After substantial group work, we prepare for casting roles.

# Individual Warm-up Exercises

## Tongue Twisters

Tongue twisters are great vocal exercises. Here are a few. Say the following tongue twisters three times fast:

- Did Chuck upchuck a chocolate chip and chick-a-cherry cola?
- Jenny drew a joyful dragon.

- Three fleas flew free.
- We read what we write.
- Peter Piper picked a peck of pickled peppers. A peck of pickled peppers Peter Piper picked. If Peter Piper picked a peck of pickled peppers, how many pickled peppers did Peter Piper pick?
- She tiptoed on tippy toes to tickle Tina's tiny nose.
- Hubert heard Henry heartily hee-haw halfway home.
- Suzy sneezed and wheezed when she saw fleas.
- Three thick tree twigs.

## Freeze Frame

Students love this exercise. Often, I use colorful scarves in the exercise. I give them a role to portray and they have a few seconds to "think, react, and act it out." After a few seconds, I shake a tambourine indicating that they have to freeze where they are. It's lightning fast and great fun as the students scramble to get into position. I start with a simple character or scene and progress to more complex roles. Here are some you can try. Get creative and add your own. The possibilities are endless.

## Some Individual Freeze Frame Roles:

- An old woman
- Girl primping herself in the mirror
- Man fixing his tie
- A boy caught stealing an apple from a neighbor's tree
- A bullfighter
- A cowboy riding his horse
- A mother cooking dinner

# Partner Warm-up Exercises

After the students become comfortable with role-playing, I have them select co-ed partners. Using the same method as above, I give them roles to portray and allow them a few seconds to "think, react, and act it out." I explain that when they are moving into their roles, they are to talk as little as possible and communicate using body language. Use the tambourine as a stop timer.

## Some Partner Freeze Frame Roles:

- Mechanic fixing his car (one is the mechanic, one is the car)
- Bus driver with a mischievous kid behind him (one is the bus driver, one is the kid)

- Mother comforting bride after being left at the altar (one is the mother, one is the bride)
- High society woman walking her dog in Central Park (one is the woman, one is the dog)
- Waiter serving irate customer (one is the waiter, one is the customer)

## Mirror, Mirror

Another great partner exercise is Mirror, Mirror. In this exercise, students are paired facing each other. One student will be the person looking into the mirror; the other will be the mirror. The person looking will make motions that the mirror copies. The pair must work together to create a seamless "mirrored" effect. I emphasize that the partners are not to touch each other. I use the tambourine to freeze partners and look at their positions. When they are finished, I switch them so that each student has a chance to play both roles. This exercise takes a great deal of concentration and focus.

## Exaggerated Mirror

Exaggerated Mirror is much like Mirror, Mirror. The difference is that the mirror must make exaggerated motions. For example, if the person looking into the mirror were smiling slightly, the mirror would be grinning from ear to ear. The mirror will wildly exaggerate every motion the person looking makes. This exercise often takes students into fits of frenzied laughter. It's fun and really serves to loosen up the group.

# Group Warm-Up Exercises

Now that the students have had interaction with each other, you can move them into group work. Divide them into small manageable groups of three or four, or create larger groups. Group work helps bond the students, establishes their work ethic, and allows them to become comfortable with the interdependence of Story Theater. Here are a couple of exercises you can try.

## Go With the Flow

With this exercise, I use music. I usually choose instrumental world music so that the students can focus on their movement. The object of this exercise is to establish group communication using silent body language. Divide the class in half and have them form two lines facing each other. Using the beat of the music, each group creates one movement that the entire group performs. The students silently communicate through body language. As they adjust to this new form of communication, the first attempt is often rough around the edges but they soon learn to work together.

## The Diorama

A diorama is a multidimensional miniature scene made with models, often created with a shoebox. In theater terms, this technique is called a tableau. Divide the class into manageable groups of 3-5 and give each group a scene to depict. Scenes from popular movies or stories work well. You can assign a historical event to begin a unit on history. Have the students create a scene within a specified time limit, freezing into position. When they are finished, have their classmates guess their scene.

# Casting Roles

When casting roles, don't choose students based on their grades. Often, I find that even a student who is a remedial reader will excel in a solo role when you set high expectations and coach them to success. Yes, students should have the ability to read the script but beyond that, it's up to you as the Story Coach to lead them to performance success.

I was coaching a class of third graders when I chose a shy girl for a storyteller's role. Charla didn't talk much but she put every bit of effort and energy into her role. When it came time to perform, Charla stood in front of her peers and told the story with a clear voice, completely in control. Her mother watched with tears in her eyes. Later, her mother approached me and said that Charla's role as a storyteller changed her life. She now had more confidence and spoke up more often. Through the risk we both took—Charla as the performer and I as the coach—Charla developed self-confidence and poise. I learned as much from her as she did from me.

For the roles of storytellers and other characters, choose students you feel will take the role seriously and try their best. Process, not product, is the most important element in Story Theater. Give students who are not usually in the limelight a chance.

Sometimes, you will find that there are some students who wanted to be a storyteller but did not receive the role. They might be reluctant to perform in the chorus. Emphasize that success depends on the group and that every line is vital. The storytellers are the cooks and the chorus is the spice. Without either contribution, the recipe for the story falls flat.

# Coaching

As the story coach, the use of praise and an atmosphere of mutual respect are very important for success. Here are some tips for successful coaching:

- When coaching the students, give suggestions rather than telling them how to perform their part. For example, instead of "Johnny, say it like this," try "Johnny, what do you think your character would sound like if he were angry?"

- When praising students, praise specific examples. "Johnny, I like the way you used your body as well as your voice to portray the bear." This will bolster the student's confidence in his abilities.

- If a student is having trouble with his part, speak to the student in private. If the student refuses to perform in front of his peers, respect his wishes. Forcing a student to perform when he is not ready can have severe psychological repercussions. If the part must be reassigned, do so without a lot of fanfare.

- When students have trouble remembering their lines, offer quiet story prompts. Sometimes signals or hand motions can jog a student's memory.

I have had students with behavioral difficulties absolutely shine in performance. The great thing about storytelling and Story Theater is that it allows students creative success. All it takes is one step up the ladder of success to initiate even more. Students will often rise to the challenge if you set high, yet reasonable expectations.

# Rehearsals

Rehearsals allow the students to work through their fears and perfect their presentations. For many students, stage fright or lack of self-confidence is the biggest inhibitor to performance success. Often, they are afraid of "messing up" in front of their peers. Assure them that you will help them with reminder lines and prompts.

The other inhibitor to performance success is inadequate preparation. When the students know exactly what to expect, they are more confident in their roles. Some elements to practice:

- Story openings and closings
- Students' positioning on the stage
- Entrances and exits
- Microphone usage

Talk openly with the class about ways to counteract stage fright including:

- Taking deep, relaxing breaths
- Warming up with exercises to get the blood moving
- Visualizing the story and working through any mistakes
- Pausing for a moment to collect their thoughts if they blank out

Work with the students as often as possible, allowing them to "tweak" their performance and to tighten up their timing as a group. If rehearsal time as a group is limited, send the scripts home with the students and have them practice their roles with a story buddy. The buddy may be a parent, a sibling, even a classmate.

In gymnastics, there is a saying, "Stick your landing." In storytelling, it works much the same way. Let the students know that even if the details are not word perfect, "stick your ending." Finish with confidence. The audience will respond positively.

# Simple Costume Ideas

Simple costumes and props can enhance the visual presentation of the stories. One of my favorite props/costume piece is a 36-inch scarf. Scarves are very lightweight and come in a variety of colors. They can be configured into a number of simple costumes including:

- Skirts
- Head Scarves

- Shawls
- Turbans
- Bandanas
- Neckties
- Togas
- Jewelry
- Coats
- Blankets
- Hats
- Wedding Veils

In addition, the scarves can also be shaped into simple props. I have had students turn them into bananas, balls, leashes, and flowers. The use of the scarves is limited only by the imagination!

Other simple costume ideas include necklaces made of yarn that hold nametags or laminated pictures of the animals or characters found in the stories. Hats, aprons, and simple objects that are mentioned in the stories also make great props. Remember, the emphasis is on the telling of the story, not on elaborate props or costumes. The beauty of Story Theater is twofold. It is easy for you and students thrive in the simplicity of the process.

# Presentation Tips: Dramatizing the Stories

Spice up the stories by creating rhythmic chants and songs from the chorus portion of the story. In some stories, the rhythm pattern of the chorus will be apparent. In others, you can add your own tune or rhythm to create an interesting backdrop for the narration of the stories.

Often, I ask the students for suggestions. Having the active involvement of the chorus in creating their rhythm creates enthusiasm and gives them ownership of their role. I encourage them to create a tune, a rap, clapping rhythms, whatever moves their creativity as long as it fits within the context of the story. Also try adding choreographed movements that the entire chorus performs together. It adds depth to the telling of the story and enhances the presentation. Don't be afraid to experiment. While the Story Fest stories are "ready made," feel free to change the lines or adapt them for the needs of your class.

If the class is performing on stage, I sit the chorus in two rows of chairs. The storytellers stand just behind them and walk up to a microphone set up to the side. If the class is performing on the floor, the chorus sits on the floor with the storytellers standing behind them. Again, the microphone is nearby for easy access by the storytellers.

When working with the storytellers, encourage them to say their parts clearly. Voice inflection and tone are very important in the storyteller's performance. Even without great movement, the storyteller can convey drama and emotion in the story with effective use of the voice and facial expressions.

# Management and Organization Tips

If you are a drama teacher working with several classes, you may find it helpful to create a binder with tabbed sections for each grade. The tabs organize the stories you are using for each grade. Here are some tips for organizing your binder.

- Sheet protectors help preserve your copies of the scripts.
- When you are casting roles, write each student's first and last name above the storyteller's role they are playing on your copy of the script. Also write the teacher's name and grade at the top of your script.
- Make personal notes in the margin of your script(s) and keep them in the sheet protectors of your binder.
- Keep extra copies of scripts in a folder in your binder for the inevitable moment a student left a script at home.

When passing out scripts to the students:

- Student's Name. Have the student write their name on their scripts as soon as they receive them. If not, they tend to dispute over which script belongs to whom.
- Teacher's Name and grade. When working with several classes have them write their teacher's name and grade on the script.

# Coordinating a Story Fest

While these scripts are great for in-class use, creating a grade-wide or school-wide Story Fest allows the student storytellers to share their efforts with an appreciative audience. Grade-wide Story Fests, where each class performs for their peers, develops an atmosphere of respect and support because each student performs during the Story Fest.

Another option is to have the class perform for lower grades. The younger students look up to the older students and the older students come away with a sense of accomplishment.

Still another alternative is to perform a Family Night Story Fest, where parents, grandparents, and other family members are invited. In this scenario, students stand proudly before their families in anticipation of their performance.

Once you have decided on your Story Fest, you will need to work out these details:

- Location of performance. Wherever you perform—cafeteria, gym, library, or auditorium—be sure to let the people in charge of that space know ahead of time. They will appreciate the advance notice and can help with preparation.
- Schedule. Coordinate scheduling with everyone involved, including other teachers, administration, staff, and parents.
- Parents. If parents are invited, send notes home. Creating a colorful invitation sets the tone for a festive mood.

- Costumes. Bring along extra costume pieces/props for the students who show up without one.

- Space. Be sure that the space is set up for the performance well before the performance.

- Announcements. Write up a blurb and give it to the morning announcer to remind students and publicize the event.

The fact that each student is performing in front of a live audience is a huge accomplishment. Following the performance, reward the students' efforts by hosting a reception. In addition, stickers or certificates are great rewards for a job well done. In the end, it's the process that matters most. Allowing the students "room to grow" and encouraging them to success is the best role a Story Coach can take. Have fun and don't forget to videotape! These are lasting memories, for you and your students.

# Crafting Story Theater Scripts

## Key Ingredients for Story Theater

My favorite place to look for stories to turn into story theater scripts is the 398.2 section of the library. Folklore, mythology, and legends are a vast resource of public domain tales waiting to be retold. I look for stories that have a timeless quality, filled with universal messages and life lessons that do not need obvious articulation. To adapt stories for Story Theater, the key ingredients are:

- Solid, simple plots
- Timeless and universal message
- One or two main characters
- Repeating action

## Selecting Stories

I often look at stories that can be found in more than one culture. If a story has migrated into another culture, it means that the story has a universal appeal. Most of our familiar favorites, *Cinderella* and *Beauty and the Beast*, for example, can be found in several cultures around the world.

Because the stories should work with a wide age range and within a limited time frame, choose stories that have uncomplicated plots and solid characters. Characters with familiarity work well. Animals, the unlikely hero, the fool, the prince, and the princess are all characters generally known by students. An epic tale such as *The Iliad* would be a difficult story to translate into this story theater process because of the complex plot and the large number of characters involved in the story.

## The Rule of Three

Seek out stories that have repeating action. Three is usually the magic number. For example, in *The Three Bears*, the bears first notice the difference in their porridge bowls, then their chairs, and finally their beds. There is repeating action in that story at least three times. This becomes the crux of how the story chorus and audience participation is developed.

# Creating the Chorus

When creating the chorus in audience participation stories and Story Theater, you can employ a number of methods to execute the repeating action:

- Rhythm

- Rhyme

- Chants

- Music

- Nonsensical language (lickity-split)

- Sound effects (Chew! Chomp!)

Keep the chorus at two to four lines to maintain its simplicity. This helps particularly since you are working with a group of kids who have to vocalize simultaneously. Keep in mind that the lines of the chorus do not always have to rhyme. I often use rhyme because I like its lyrical sound and I also find that rhyme aids the students' retention of the material. However, rhythm and non-rhyming chants also work well because of their pattern and regularity. The key is consistency when creating the chorus.

# Putting It All Together

Tip or hint to the Story Theater chorus that their part is coming by keeping a consistent "trip" word or phrase integrated throughout the story. When the word or phrase is vocalized, it acts as a cue for the chorus or audience to do their part.

There are many ways to retell traditional folktales. When creating your story theater scripts, be sure to read them out loud to a few story buddies of your own. This will allow you to test the language and its effect on potential audiences. Creating a story theater script for your class is a great way to introduce new elements into your lesson plan or unit. If you are studying Germany, for example, take a look at stories collected by the Brothers Grimm.

Soliciting the input of your students to shape a story script is a fantastic way to create a story theater that belongs to the entire class. In addition to performing the piece, they will also garner experience in script writing, sequencing, and problem solving. One of the greatest rewards in life is to see your hard work come to fruition. For students, seeing their creativity go from the brain to the page to the stage is a satisfying experience that many of them remember for years to come.

# Story Theater
# Scripts

# World Folktales

# Sausage Nose

## Sweden

| | |
|---|---|
| **Storyteller 1:** | There was once an old woman who was alone in her old house while her husband was out chopping wood in the forest. A young woman came knocking at the door asking to borrow a frying pan. |
| **Old Woman:** | Yes, you may borrow my frying pan. I hardly ever use it anyway. |
| **Storyteller 2:** | So the young woman took the frying pan thanking the old woman. A few days later, the young woman returned the frying pan and told the old woman that because of her kindness she could have three wishes. |
| **Chorus:** | One wish, two wishes, three wishes for you. |
| | Use them wisely or you'll end up a fool. |
| **Storyteller 2:** | The old woman thought about her wishes and wanted something tasty for dinner. She made her first wish. |
| **Old Woman:** | With my three wishes |
| | I wish for something delicious… |
| | A big fat sausage! |
| **Storyteller 3:** | A delicious sausage appeared in the middle of the table. The old woman was so happy. Then her husband came home. She told him the story and showed him the sausage. He was not happy. |
| **Old Man:** | You mean you could have wished for anything in the world and you wished for a sausage? How foolish! |
| **Chorus:** | One wish, two wishes, three wishes for you. |

Use them wisely or you'll end up a fool.

**Old Man:** I wish that sausage were sticking to your nose!

**Storyteller 4:** Much to the old woman's dismay, the fat sausage stuck to the end of her nose and she couldn't get it off. She and her husband tried to pull it off but it was no use. The sausage was stuck.

**Old Woman:** You have to do something! I can't live the rest of my life with a sausage on the end of my nose!

**Storyteller 5:** So the old man thought about it. He could wish for a new computer or a new flat screen TV or even a brand new car. But his wife was not happy and no man can live a good life when his wife is not happy. So he wished…

**Chorus:** One wish, two wishes, three wishes for you.

Use them wisely or you'll end up a fool.

**Old Man:** I wish for the sausage to be gone from the end of my wife's nose.

**Storyteller 6:** In an instant, the sausage dropped onto a plate and the old woman's nose was back to normal. She was happy again. And because she was happy, he was happy. And isn't that what wishes are supposed to do?

**Chorus:** One wish, two wishes, three wishes for you.

Use them wisely or you'll end up a fool.

# The Wee, Wee Mannie
# and the
# Big, Big Coo

## Scotland

---

**Storyteller 1:** Once there was a wee, wee mannie and he had a big, big coo. One fine morning, he went out with his pail to draw some milk. But the big, big coo swished her tail, kicked up her heels, and knocked the pail out of his hands. The wee, wee mannie cried out:

**Chorus:** What's a wee, wee mannie to do?

With such a big contrary coo?

**Storyteller 2:** So he went to his mother's house and said, "Mother, Coo won't stand still and wee, wee mannie can't milk big, big coo!" So Mother took the pail to the big, big coo said, "Stay still!" But the big, big coo swished her tail, kicked up her heels and knocked the pail out of her hands. The wee, wee mannie cried out:

**Chorus:** What's a wee, wee mannie to do?

With such a big contrary coo?

**Storyteller 3:** So they went to his sister's house and said, "Coo won't stand still and wee, wee mannie can't milk big, big coo!" So Sister took the pail to the big, big coo said, "Stay still!" But the big, big coo swished her tail, kicked up her heels and knocked the pail out of her hands. The wee, wee mannie cried out:

**Chorus:**   What's a wee, wee mannie to do?

With such a big contrary coo?

**Storyteller 4:**   Mother said, "It seems that big, big coo does the opposite of what you ask her to do. Why don't we try something new? So wee, wee mannie said to coo, "Big, big coo, please swish your tail, kick up your heels, and knock this pail out of my hands!" And guess what?

**Chorus:**   Big, big coo stood still.

**Storyteller 5:**   Wee, wee mannie milked big, big coo and shared fresh milk with his mother and sister. And the big, big coo never acted like that again—until the next time!

# The Turtle Who Could Not Stop Talking

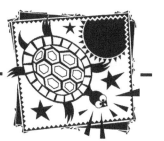

East India

---

| | |
|---|---|
| **Storyteller 1:** | Once a turtle who lived in a muddy little pond liked to talk to everyone. |
| **Chorus:** | He talked and talked and talked and talked... |
| **Storyteller 2:** | One day, two beautiful geese came by. They asked, "How would you like to fly?" "Of course," said Turtle and |
| **Chorus:** | He talked and talked and talked and talked... |
| **Storyteller 3:** | One goose cried, "If you want to go, you must quit chattering so. Grab on to this stick with your mouth and don't let go!" "Of course," said Turtle and |
| **Chorus:** | He talked and talked and talked and talked... |
| **Storyteller 4:** | Finally, Turtle bit the stick and the geese took flight. Soon he was flying high in the sky. But down below, he saw some friends. He opened his mouth to say a few words and |
| **Chorus:** | He fell and fell and fell and fell |
| **Chorus:** | KA-THUD! |
| **Storyteller 5:** | Turtle landed on the ground and on his back. If you look at him now, you can see the cracks! He is much quieter these days. For Turtle has learned to change his ways! |
| **Storyteller 6:** | Too much talking can get you into trouble! |

# The Little Red Hen

## England

Storyteller 1: Twice as long as long ago, there lived a little red hen. She was looking for some food in the farmyard when she found some grains of wheat. She saw her friends and asked, "Now who will help me plant the wheat?"

Chorus: "Not I," said the Dog,

"Not I," said the Cat,

"Not I," said the Duck.

And that was that.

Storyteller 2: "I'll plant it myself," and she did. When the wheat grew tall, the little red hen asked her friends, "Now who will help me cut the wheat?"

Chorus: "Not I," said the Dog,

"Not I," said the Cat,

"Not I," said the Duck.

And that was that.

Storyteller 3: "I'll cut it myself," and she did. When the wheat was cut, the little red hen asked her friends, "Now who will help me grind the wheat?"

Chorus: "Not I," said the Dog,

"Not I," said the Cat,

"Not I," said the Duck.

And that was that.

**Storyteller 4:** "I'll grind it myself," and she did. When the wheat was ground, the little red hen asked her friends, "Now who will help me bake the bread?"

**Chorus:** "Not I," said the Dog,

"Not I," said the Cat,

"Not I," said the Duck.

And that was that.

**Storyteller 5:** "I'll bake it myself," and she did. When the bread was baked, the little red hen asked her friends, "Now who will help me eat the bread?"

**Chorus:** "I will," said the Dog,

"I will," said the Cat,

"I will," said the Duck.

And that was that.

**Storyteller 6:** "No, you won't," said the little red hen. "None of you helped me plant the wheat, cut the wheat, grind the wheat, or bake the bread! I'll eat it myself," and she did!

# The Battle of the Firefly and the Apes

## Philippines

| | |
|---|---|
| **Storyteller 1:** | In the land of the 7,000 islands, there lived a firefly. One evening, the firefly took his little lamp to visit a friend. Along the way, he met an ape. The ape said, |
| **Ape:** | Firefly, why do you always carry a light? |
| **Firefly:** | I carry a light so that I can see the mosquitoes and keep out of their way. |
| **Storyteller 2:** | The large ape made fun of the firefly. |
| **Chorus:** | Little firefly is afraid of mosquitoes. |
| | He carries a lantern wherever he goes. |
| **Firefly:** | I am not afraid of mosquitoes. I just like to mind my own business and keep out of theirs. |
| **Storyteller 3:** | But the ape didn't believe the firefly. He went to his ape friends and told them about the firefly. He told them that firefly was a coward. |
| **Chorus:** | Little firefly is afraid of mosquitoes. |
| | He carries a lantern wherever he goes. |
| **Storyteller 4:** | Firefly soon heard that ape told his friends that firefly was a coward. Firefly visited ape and said, |
| **Firefly:** | Why did you tell everyone I was a coward? Tomorrow, come to plaza and in front of everyone, I will prove I am not a coward. |

24

**Ape:** Are you offering to fight me? Who will you bring to help you?

**Firefly:** I shall come alone.

**Ape:** Fine. Come by yourself. I am going to bring all of my friends. We shall see what happens to you if you dare to come alone!

**Storyteller 5:** The next day, the ape and his ape friends gathered in the plaza. They each carried large clubs and placed themselves in a line, with the great ape at the head of the line. Firefly came alone. The apes chanted,

**Chorus:** Little firefly is afraid of mosquitoes.

He carries a lantern wherever he goes.

**Storyteller 6:** The little firefly flew swiftly over the great ape's nose. The ape that stood in line next to him swung his club and knocked the great ape silly, hitting him squarely on the nose.

**Storyteller 7:** Then the firefly hurried to the second ape's nose. His friend next to him brought his club down and knocked him silly. This continued all the way down the line until each one of the apes lay flat on the ground.

**Storyteller 8:** The apes lay on the ground in shame, knowing that the firefly had defeated them with cleverness and wit. The firefly danced over the apes carrying his lantern proudly.

**Chorus:** Little firefly's bravery shines bright.

His lantern lights the darkest night.

# The Ugly Duckling

Denmark

**Storyteller 1:** One Spring, a mother duck sat on her eggs and they began to hatch. Beautiful yellow chicks came out of their shells.

**Storyteller 2:** She saw a large egg she didn't see before. When the egg cracked, a clumsy gray bird with a long neck fell out.

**Storyteller 3:** The mother duck said, "What an ugly duckling!" The other chicks cried out,

**Chorus:** What an ugly duckling! What an ugly duckling!

**Storyteller 4:** The gray bird felt bad and walked to the pond. He saw some beautiful white birds on the water. He wanted to be like them.

**Storyteller 5:** The gray bird would come to the pond often to watch the beautiful white birds. Time passed and the gray bird grew bigger.

**Storyteller 6:** One day, he noticed his reflection in the water. He was no longer an ugly duckling! He turned into a beautiful white bird.

**Storyteller 7:** Some children saw him and came running to the pond. They cried out,

**Chorus:** What a beautiful swan! What a beautiful swan!

**Storyteller 7:** We all transform with time.

# Why the Bear Is Stumpy-Tailed

## Norway

| | |
|---|---|
| **Storyteller 1:** | Bear has big sharp teeth, long sharp claws, shaggy brown fur, and a long bushy tail. Well, he might not have a long, bushy tail now, but there was a time when he did. |
| **Storyteller 2:** | He loved his bushy tail and swished it every chance he got. Swish. Swish. Swish. (Teller swishes backside back and forth) |
| **Storyteller 3:** | Bear had a neighbor who also had a big, bushy tail. His name was Fox. One day, crafty Fox came around the corner with a string of fish in his hand. Bear said, "Howdy, Fox. Those fish look really good." |
| **Fox:** | Yes they do, don't they? I am going to fry them, and roast them, and bake them, and broil them. Then I'm going to EAT them! |
| **Storyteller 4:** | Bear eyed the fish hungrily. He used his big bear bully tactics and towered over Fox, "Fox, give me some of those fish." Fox backed up and said, |
| **Fox:** | Whoa, big guy. I tell you what. Instead of me giving these fish to you, why don't I show you how you can catch your own? With your long, bushy tail, you're sure to catch twice as many as me. |
| **Storyteller 5:** | Bear grinned at that thought—twice as many fish as Fox. "Okay," said Bear, "What do I do?" |

27

**Chorus:** Swish your tail to the left.

Swish your tail to the right.

Then settle yourself in the ice hole.

And wait for the fish to bite.

**Fox:** Before long, you'll start to feel tingling in your tail; that's the fish biting. But don't get up yet. Wait until you don't feel anything anymore; that means your tail is heavy with fish. Then pull real hard and you will have a tail full of fish!

**Storyteller 6:** Bear was so excited. "Fish. Fish. Fish. I'm going to fry them, and roast them, and bake them and broil them. And then I am going to eat them! And I will have twice as many as you, Fox!"

**Storyteller 7:** Fox laughed as Bear set off for the ice hole. "That's right, Bear. Twice as many." Bear thought he'd better remember what Fox told him so he chanted to himself.

**Chorus:** Swish my tail to the left.

Swish my tail to the right.

Then settle myself in the ice hole.

And wait for the fish to bite.

**Storyteller 8:** Soon, Bear came to a nice ice hole. He remembered what Fox told him to do.

**Chorus:** Swish my tail to the left.

Swish my tail to the right.

Then settle myself in the ice hole.

And wait for the fish to bite.

**Storyteller 9:** And he did exactly that. As he sat, he felt tingling in his tail. "Good," he thought to himself, "the fish are biting." Then he didn't feel anything in his tail; his tail felt rather heavy.

**Storyteller 10:** "Good," he said, "my tail is heavy with fish! I'll have twice as many fish as Fox. And I'm going to fry them, and roast them, and bake them, and broil them and then I am going to eat them! It's time to pull up the fish!" So bear began pulling.

**Chorus:** He pulled to the left.

He pulled to the right.

He yanked real hard

and then yelled, "Ay yi yi!"

**Storyteller 11:** Bear pulled so hard that his long, bushy tail stayed in the ice. To this day, Bear still has a stumpy tail. Since then, grumpy Bear has slept through the winter and has had to "grin and bear" his fate. And that, my friends, is the end of Bear's tale.

# Aesop Fables

# The Tortoise and the Hare

| | |
|---|---|
| **Storyteller 1:** | A hare once made fun of Tortoise's slow gait. The Tortoise laughed and replied, "Though you may be as swift as the wind, I could beat you in a race." Hare answered, "Bring it on." |
| **Storyteller 2:** | So a bet was made and the race was set. Because Hare was so confident he would win, he began to play around. Meanwhile... |
| **Chorus:** | Tortoise never wavered from the race. |
| | He kept on going at a steady pace. |
| **Storyteller 3:** | Hare was so confident he would win, he began nibbling on juicy grass and picking flowers. Meanwhile... |
| **Chorus:** | Tortoise never wavered from the race. |
| | He kept on going at a steady pace. |
| **Storyteller 4:** | Hare was so confident he would win, he decided to take a nap. Meanwhile... |
| **Chorus:** | Tortoise never wavered from the race. |
| | He kept on going at a steady pace. |
| **Storyteller 5:** | When hare awoke, to his surprise he found that Tortoise was approaching the finish line. He dashed as swift as the wind but it was too late. Slow Tortoise had won the race. |
| **Chorus:** | Tortoise never wavered from the race. |
| | He kept on going at a steady pace. |
| **Storyteller 6:** | Always keep a steady pace and you will surely win the race. |

# The Country Mouse and the City Mouse

**Storyteller 1:** Once there was a country mouse that lived a very simple and peaceful life. One day, his friend from the city came to visit.

**Storyteller 2:** The country mouse only had a crumb of bread and a stale piece of cheese to give the city mouse. They sat down and ate.

**Chorus:** They nibbled and nibbled and nibbled and nibbled.

**Storyteller 3:** When they finished eating, City Mouse said, "You eat like a beggar. Come to the city and I will show you fine dining."

**Storyteller 4:** Country mouse agreed and they traveled to the city. When they arrived, City Mouse brought Country Mouse into a large dining room.

**Storyteller 5:** Delicious food covered a huge table. There were big loaves of bread and large pieces of cheese.

**Chorus:** They nibbled and nibbled and nibbled and nibbled.

**Storyteller 6:** When they were finished, City Mouse bragged about his fine life. Suddenly, a great big cat appeared and began chasing the two mice.

**Chorus:** They ran and ran and ran and ran!

**Storyteller 7:** Country Mouse waved goodbye to his friend and ran out the door. He cried out, "I would rather live a simple life with less than live a dangerous life with more!"

# The Ant and the Grasshopper

| | |
|---|---|
| **Storyteller 1:** | It was springtime and Grasshopper was busy singing a song. Soon, Ant came by dragging some food behind him. Ant was: |
| **Chorus:** | Pushing and pulling and tugging and lugging. |
| **Storyteller 2:** | Grasshopper said, "Why don't you stop working and play with me?" Ant answered, "I am too busy preparing for the winter." "Suit yourself," sang Grasshopper. |
| **Storyteller 3:** | Spring turned into summer and Grasshopper was busy singing a song. Ant came by dragging some food behind him. Ant was: |
| **Chorus:** | Pushing and pulling and tugging and lugging. |
| **Storyteller 4:** | Grasshopper said, "Why don't you stop working and play with me?" Ant answered, "I am too busy preparing for the winter." "Suit yourself," sang Grasshopper. |
| **Storyteller 5:** | Well, summer turned into fall and Grasshopper was busy singing a song. Ant came by dragging some food behind him. Ant was: |
| **Chorus:** | Pushing and pulling and tugging and lugging. |
| **Storyteller 6:** | Grasshopper said, "Why don't you stop working and play with me?" Ant answered, "I am too busy preparing for the winter." "Suit yourself," sang Grasshopper. |

**Storyteller 7:**   Fall turned into winter. Because Grasshopper sang all year long, he didn't gather any food. He lay in the snow cold and hungry. When Ant came by and saw Grasshopper, he took pity. Ant said, "I'll take you in tonight, Grasshopper, but you must sing for your supper!"

**Storyteller 8:**   If you don't work hard, you could find yourself out in the cold!

# The Frog and the Ox

**Storyteller 1:** A little frog was nearly trampled by a big ox. The little frog hopped home to tell the biggest frog in the pond his story.

**Storyteller 2:** The little frog said, "It was a great big beast that nearly trampled me beneath its feet!"

**Storyteller 3:** The big frog, who was very vain, said, "Was he this big?" and he puffed himself up as much as he could.

**Chorus:** "Ribbit, Ribbit, he was much bigger than that!

Ribbit, Ribbit, he was fatter than fat!"

**Storyteller 4:** The big frog said, "Was he this big?" and he puffed himself up even bigger than before!

**Chorus:** "Ribbit, Ribbit, he was much bigger than that!

Ribbit, Ribbit, he was fatter than fat!"

**Storyteller 5:** The big frog couldn't even reach half the ox's size. He tried in vain with all his might. He puffed himself up as big as a balloon until...

**Chorus:** POP!

**Storyteller 6:** If you puff yourself up enough, you will explode with your own greatness.

# The Boy Who Cried Wolf

**Storyteller 1:** A shepherd boy tended a flock of sheep not far from a village. He decided to play a trick on the villagers. He cried out:

**Chorus:** "Villagers, villagers, danger is near

A Wolf! A Wolf! Come quickly here!"

**Storyteller 2:** The villagers thought the boy and the sheep were in danger. They ran quickly to the shepherd only to find him laughing.

**Storyteller 3:** They warned the boy against his foolishness and went home. The next day, the boy decided to play his trick again. He cried out:

**Chorus:** "Villagers, villagers, danger is near

A Wolf! A Wolf! Come quickly here!"

**Storyteller 4:** Once again, the villagers thought the boy and the sheep were in danger. They ran quickly to the shepherd only to find him laughing.

**Storyteller 5:** They warned the boy against his foolishness and went home. The next day, the boy saw a wolf. He cried out:

**Chorus:** "Villagers, villagers, danger is near

A Wolf! A Wolf! Come quickly here!"

**Storyteller 6:** But no villagers came. His cries fell upon deaf ears. The villagers were tired of his foolish tricks. His sheep were left to the mercy of the wolf.

**Storyteller 7:** Even when liars tell the truth, they are never believed.

# The Lion and the Mouse

**Storyteller 1:** Ssssshh. In the jungle the lion was sleeping. He was taking a nap. By and by, a little mouse, not watching where she was walking stepped on lion's nose and woke him up. He roared:

**Lion:** ROAR!

**Storyteller 2:** He wrapped his paws around the little mouse and said, "You should never wake a lion from his cat nap." The little mouse said, "I'm sorry, Mr. Lion. If you let me go, I promise to be your friend and help you when you are in need. Please let me go."

**Chorus:** But the lion shook his head no and wouldn't let go.

**Storyteller 3:** The lion said, "You! Friend to a great beast like myself! Ha! Never!" The mouse said again, "Please, Mr. Lion, I can be your friend. Let me go."

**Chorus:** But the lion shook his head no and wouldn't let go.

**Storyteller 4:** So the little mouse did something different. She began to whine. "Pleeeeeeease let me goooooooooooooooo." She was making such a racket that the Lion let go and covered both of his ears with his paws. The little mouse scampered off.

**Storyteller 5:** A few days later, the little mouse was walking through the jungle when she heard a strange noise. It sounded like a sick kitty cat moaning and groaning.

**Lion:** Meow. Meow. Moan. Groan.

**Storyteller 6:**   The lion was caught in a hunter's net. When the lion saw the mouse, he begged for help. The little mouse said, "I made a promise and I will keep it. But if I help you and set you free, you must promise not to EAT me!" The lion promised.

**Storyteller 7:**   The little mouse nibbled and nibbled through the net until the lion was free. He stood up and let out a ferocious roar.

**Lion:**   ROAR!

**Storyteller 8:**   Then he reached for the mouse and without saying a word pulled her close to his mouth. She cried out, "You promised not to eat me!" Suddenly, the lion bent down and gave the mouse a great big SMOOCH on the lips.

**Chorus:**   Eeeewwww.

**Storyteller 9:**   From that time forward, the Lion and the Mouse were the best of friends and it just goes to show you that friendship comes in all shapes and sizes.

# American Folktales

# Brer Rabbit and the Tar Baby

**Storyteller 1:** Brer Rabbit was a rascally rabbit. He was always tricking folks and getting the best of them. Brer Fox was tired of it and decided he wanted to get back at Brer Rabbit. So Brer Fox mixed tar with turpentine and made an icky sticky, ooey gooey concoction. He shaped it into a person and stuck a straw hat on top. He called it the "Tar Baby."

**Storyteller 2:** It was a hot day and Brer Fox set the tar baby in the middle of the road on the way to the well. He knew that Brer Rabbit would come by soon. He hid low behind the bushes waiting for Brer Rabbit. Sure enough, Brer Rabbit came hopping down the road.

**Chorus:** Lippity-clippity. Clippity-lippity.

**Storyteller 3:** Brer Fox said, "That Brer Rabbit sure is as sassy as a jaybird" and he stayed hidden low in the bushes, watching. Brer Rabbit saw the tar baby in the middle of the road and stopped to say hello.

**Chorus:** Hello, ma'am, how're you doing today?

Nice weather we're having, wouldn't you say?

**Storyteller 4:** But the tar baby didn't say a word. She just stared at Brer Rabbit. Brer Rabbit said, "Didn't you hear a word I just said? I said…

**Chorus:** Hello, ma'am, how're you doing today?

Nice weather we're having, wouldn't you say?

41

**Storyteller 4:** But the tar baby still didn't say a word. Brer Rabbit was angry. "If you don't take off that hat and say hello good and proper, I'm going to teach you a lesson!" Still, the tar baby didn't say a word. So Brer Rabbit pulled back his right fist and swung,

**Chorus:** SMACK! Brer Rabbit's right fist got stuck.

**Storyteller 5:** Brer Fox watched from the bushes where he was hidden and began to laugh. Brer Rabbit was even angrier. "If you don't let me loose, I'm going to knock you silly!" Still, the tar baby didn't say a word. So Brer Rabbit pulled back his left fist and swung.

**Chorus:** SMACK! Brer Rabbit's left fist got stuck.

**Storyteller 6:** Brer Fox kept on watching from the bushes where he was hidden and laughed at Brer Rabbit. By now, Brer Rabbit was furious. "Let me loose before I kick the stuffing out of you!" he yelled at the tar baby. Still, the tar baby didn't say a word. So Brer Rabbit pulled back his right foot and kicked.

**Chorus:** SMACK! Brer Rabbit's right foot got stuck!

**Storyteller 7:** By this time, Brer Rabbit was good and stuck. His fur was covered with icky, sticky, ooey gooey black tar. Brer Fox couldn't take it anymore! He sprung out from behind the bushes and laughed. "Brer Rabbit, you look sort of stuck this morning! You've been acting like the boss of the plantation, tricking folks and getting the best of them. Now I got you good!"

**Storyteller 8:** Brer Rabbit couldn't loose himself because he was good and stuck. Brer Fox said, "Funny thing is, you got yourself into that mess. Let's see you get yourself out of this mess! Stay here while I get some brush pile so I can start a fire. I'm having barbecue today!"

**Storyteller 9:** Brer Rabbit said, "You can roast me but whatever you do…

**Chorus:** DON'T THROW ME IN THE BRIAR PATCH.

**Storyteller 9:** Brer Fox couldn't find any brush pile so he said, "Maybe I'll boil you. It'll be easier." Brer Rabbit said, "You can boil me but whatever you do…

**Chorus:** DON'T THROW ME IN THE BRIAR PATCH.

**Storyteller 9:** Brer Fox couldn't find any water so he said, "Maybe I'll tie you up and save you for later." Brer Rabbit said, "You can tie me up but whatever you do…

**Chorus:** DON'T THROW ME IN THE BRIAR PATCH.

**Storyteller 10:** Brer Fox couldn't find any rope so he said, "I'm going to throw you into the briar patch!" He pulled Brer Rabbit from the tar baby and flung him by his back legs into the briar patch.

**Storyteller 11:** Brer Rabbit flew into the briar patch, right into the bushes. A minute later, Brer Rabbit stuck his head out and yelled at Brer Fox. "It's too bad you lost your catch! I was born and bred in the briar patch!" He stuck out his tongue at Brer Fox and hopped away.

**Chorus:** Lippity-clippity. Clippity-lippity.

**Storyteller 12:** Brer Rabbit was a rascally rabbit. He was always tricking folks and getting the best of them. The end.

# The Gunny Wolf

**Storyteller 1:** There was once a little girl who lived with her mother in a small house by the forest. Her mother always warned her to stay away from the forest or the Gunny Wolf might get her.

**Storyteller 2:** One day, the little girl was home by herself. She saw some beautiful white flowers by the edge of the forest. Forgetting her mother's warning, she neared the woods and picked the flowers. A little further beyond, she saw pink flowers. She picked them too. Still deeper in the forest, she saw bright yellow flowers. She picked them too, singing:

**Chorus:** Tray bla. Kee wa. Kum kwa. Kee ma.

**Storyteller 3:** Suddenly, the Gunny Wolf appeared. He said, "Sing that guten, sweeten song again." So the little girl began singing.

**Chorus:** Tray bla. Kee wa. Kum kwa. Kee ma.

**Storyteller 4:** The Gunny Wolf fell asleep and the little girl began running away,

**Chorus:** Pit-a-pat. Pit-a-pat. Pit-a-pat. Pit-a-pat.

**Storyteller 4:** The Gunny Wolf woke up and began chasing the girl.

**Chorus:** Hunka-cha. Hunka-cha. Hunka-cha. Hunka-cha.

**Storyteller 5:** When he caught up to the little girl, he said, "Little girl, why for you move?" She said, "I no move." The Gunny Wolf said, "Sing that guten, sweeten song again." So the little girl began singing.

**Chorus:** Tray bla. Kee wa. Kum kwa. Kee ma.

**Storyteller 6:** The Gunny Wolf fell asleep again and once more, the little girl began running away,

**Chorus:** Pit-a-pat. Pit-a-pat. Pit-a-pat. Pit-a-pat.

**Storyteller 6:** The Gunny Wolf woke up and began chasing the girl.

**Chorus:** Hunka-cha. Hunka-cha. Hunka-cha. Hunka-cha.

**Storyteller 7:** When he caught up to the little girl, he said, "Little girl, why for you move?" She said, "I no move." The Gunny Wolf said, "Sing that guten, sweeten song again." So the little girl began singing.

**Chorus:** Tray bla. Kee wa. Kum kwa. Kee ma.

**Storyteller 8:** The Gunny Wolf fell asleep again and once more, the little girl began running away,

**Chorus:** Pit-a-pat. Pit-a-pat. Pit-a-pat. Pit-a-pat.

**Storyteller 8:** The Gunny Wolf woke up and began chasing the girl.

**Chorus:** Hunka-cha. Hunka-cha. Hunka-cha. Hunka-cha.

**Storyteller 9:** The little girl kept running with the Gunny Wolf chasing her.

**Chorus:** Pit-a-pat. Pit-a-pat. Pit-a-pat. Pit-a-pat.

**Chorus:** Hunka-cha. Hunka-cha. Hunka-cha. Hunka-cha.

**Storyteller 9:** Finally, she reached her house, opened the door, and slammed it tight.

**Chorus:** BOOM!

**Storyteller 10:** Since then, the little girl has never entered the forest and always heeds her mother's warnings.

**Chorus:** Tray bla. Kee wa. Kum kwa. Kee ma.

# Epaminondas

Storyteller 1: Epaminondas was a little boy who didn't always use common sense. He used to visit his Auntie every day. When it was time for him to go home, his auntie would give him a gift to bring to his mama.

Storyteller 1: One day, she gave Epaminondas a delicious piece of cake. Epaminondas said, "Thank you, auntie" and he held the cake tight in his hands as he traveled home.

Storyteller 2: When he got home, the cake was a squishy mess oozing through his fingers. His mama asked him, "What do you have there, son?" He stuck out his hands and answered, "Cake, mama!"

Chorus: His mama said, "Epaminondas! You ain't got the sense you were born with!"

Storyteller 2: His mama said, "That's no way to carry a cake. Next time, wrap it up in some leaves and carry it home on your head." Epaminondas answered, "Yes, mama."

Storyteller 3: The next day, Epaminondas went to visit his auntie. When it was time for him to go home, his auntie handed him some butter for his mama. Epaminondas said, "Thank you, auntie" and he wrapped the butter in leaves and put it on top of his head. But it was a very hot day and the butter began to… melt!

Storyteller 3: The butter dripped down his face and his neck. When his mama saw him, she asked, "What do you have there, son?" He smiled and licked his lips, "Butter, mama!"

Chorus: His mama said, "Epaminondas! You ain't got the sense you were born with!"

**Storyteller 4:**   His mama said, "That's no way to carry butter. Next time, put it in a bucket of cool water and carry it home." Epaminondas answered, "Yes, mama."

**Storyteller 4:**   The next day, Epaminondas went to visit his auntie. When it was time for him to go home, he auntie gave him a little kitten to bring home. Epaminondas said, "Thank you, auntie," and he filled a bucket with some cool water, placed the kitten inside, and carried it home. The water sloshed inside the bucket.

**Storyteller 5:**   When Epaminondas arrived home, the poor kitty was soaking wet and looked like a little rat! "Mewwww," it said pitifully. When his mama saw the bucket and the wet rat, she asked, "What do you have there, son?" He smiled and handed her the bucket. Epaminondas answered, "A kitty, mama!"

**Chorus:**   His mama said, "Epaminondas! You ain't got the sense you were born with!"

**Storyteller 5:**   His mama said, "That's no way to carry home a kitten. Next time, you must tie a string around its neck and walk home, with the kitten following behind you." Epaminondas answered, "Yes, mama."

**Storyteller 6:**   The next day, Epaminondas went to visit his auntie. When it was time for him to go home, he auntie gave him a big ham to bring home. Epaminondas said, "Thank you, auntie," and he tied a piece of string around it and began dragging it behind him. By the time he reached home, the ham was covered in dirt, leaves and mud!

**Storyteller 7:**   When his mama saw what Epaminondas was dragging, she asked, "What do you have there, son? He smiled and said, "Ham, mama!"

**Chorus:**   His mama said, "Epaminondas! You ain't got the sense you were born with!"

**Storyteller 7:**   His mama said, "That's no way to bring home the ham. Next time, you must wrap your arms around it and carry it home like that." Epaminondas said, "Yes, mama!"

**Storyteller 8:**   The next day, Epaminondas went to visit his auntie. When it was time for him to go home, he auntie gave him a big donkey to bring home. Epaminondas said, "Thank you, auntie," and he wrapped his arms around the donkey and tried to carry it home, just like his mama said. But the donkey was too heavy! He heaved and pulled but the donkey would not budge. Finally, Epaminondas sat down by the side of the road and cried.

**Storyteller 9:**   Meanwhile, it was getting dark and Epaminondas' mama was getting worried. He had not yet returned home. So she went looking for him. Sure enough, she found him sitting by the side of the road crying, right next to the donkey.

**Storyteller 10:**   His mama said, "What do you have there, son?" Epaminondas answered, "A donkey, mama. But I couldn't carry it home like you said. I'm sorry." His mama wrapped her arms around him tight and said softly, "Epaminondas, you ain't got the sense you were born with but you sure got a big heart. Come on son, let's go home."

**Storyteller 11:**   So she picked up Epaminondas and set him atop the donkey. And the donkey carried Epaminondas all the way home.

# The Chicken and the Librarian

| | |
|---|---|
| **Storyteller 1:** | One day, a chicken came into the library, walked to the desk, flapped her wings and clucked, |
| **Chicken:** | "Bok, bok, bok, bok, bok, bok." |
| **Storyteller 2:** | The librarian, Mrs. Miller, gave the chicken a puzzled look. What could a chicken want? Mrs. Miller guessed that the chicken wanted books. So she selected a few titles, tucked the books under the chicken's wings, and watched as the chicken left the library. |
| **Storyteller 3:** | A few minutes later, the chicken returned. She dropped the books on the desk, flapped her wings and clucked, |
| **Chicken:** | "Bok, bok, bok, bok, bok, bok." |
| **Storyteller 4:** | Mrs. Miller was again puzzled. The chicken did not appear to care for the books she selected. So she picked out a few more books, tucked them under the chicken's wings, and watched as the chicken again left the library. |
| **Storyteller 5:** | A few minutes later, the chicken returned. She dropped the books on the desk, flapped her wings and clucked, |
| **Chicken:** | "Bok, bok, bok, bok, bok, bok." |
| **Storyteller 6:** | Again, it seemed as though the chicken did not care for the books. So Mrs. Miller picked out a few more books and tucked them under the chicken's wings. But this time, she decided to follow the chicken. |

**Storyteller 7:** The chicken led Mrs. Miller to a small pond where a large bullfrog was sitting by the water. The chicken began handing the books to the frog, one at a time, but each time she did, he cried out:

**Frog:** Read it! Read it! Read it!

# Jack Seeks His Fortune

| | |
|---|---|
| **Storyteller 1:** | In a land of green rolling hills, there once lived a boy named Jack. One day, Jack decided that it was time for him to make his fortune. He began traveling down the road. He had not gone very far when he met a sad old donkey. The donkey said |
| **Chorus:** | Hee haw, I don't know what to do |
| | My master doesn't want me. Can I go with you? |
| **Storyteller 2:** | Jack said, "Sure!" And the two set off together. They journeyed down the road a little ways when they met a sad old cow. The cow said |
| **Chorus:** | Moo moo, I don't know what to do |
| | My master doesn't want me. Can I go with you? |
| **Storyteller 3:** | Jack said, "Sure!" And the three set off together. They journeyed down the road a little ways when they met a sad old dog. The dog said |
| **Chorus:** | Arf arf, I don't know what to do |
| | My master doesn't want me. Can I go with you? |
| **Storyteller 4:** | Jack said, "Sure!" And the four set off together. They journeyed down the road a little ways when they met a sad old cat. The cat said |
| **Chorus:** | Meow meow, I don't know what to do |
| | My master doesn't want me. Can I go with you? |

**Storyteller 5:** Jack said, "Sure!" And the five set off together. They journeyed down the road a little ways when they met a sad old rooster. The rooster said

**Chorus:** Cock-a-doodle-do, I don't know what to do

My master doesn't want me. Can I go with you?

**Storyteller 6:** Jack said, "Sure!" And they all set off together. They journeyed until it was nearly dark. Then Jack spotted a house. He told the animals, "Sssssshhhh" as he peeked in through the window. Much to his surprise, he saw a gang of robbers counting their gold!

**Storyteller 7:** Jack had a bright idea. He said, "When I wave my hand, make as much noise as you can." When the animals were ready, Jack gave the signal. The donkey brayed, the cow mooed, the dog barked, the cat meowed, and the rooster crowed. Together, they made such an awful racket that the noise scared away the robbers and they left behind all of their—gold!

**Storyteller 8:** Jack and the animals went inside the house and made themselves comfortable. Then Jack began to worry that the robbers would come back. So he came up with another plan. He put the donkey near the door, the cow by the fireplace, the dog under the table, the cat in the rocking chair, and the rooster on a beam at the top. Finally, Jack fell asleep.

**Storyteller 9:** Jack was right. The robbers returned. They decided to look for their gold. They sent one of their men inside the house. When the robber came in, the rooster crowed loudly, the cat scratched him, the dog bit his leg, the cow slapped him with his tail, and the donkey kicked him out the door. He ran back to the other robbers and they never returned to the house again.

**Storyteller 10:** Jack and the animals lived in peace and contentment for the rest of their days. Jack made his fortune, but the best fortune of all was his friends.

# Sody Sallyraytus

| | |
|---|---|
| **Storyteller 1:** | Once there lived a grandpa, a grandma, a little boy, a little girl and their pet squirrel. One day, the grandma wanted to bake some biscuits but she was out of sody sallyraytus: baking soda. So she sent the little boy to the store. He bought the sody and sang a song home: |
| **Chorus:** | Sody sallyraytus, lickity-split |
| | Grandma's going to bake some biscuits with it. |
| **Storyteller 2:** | He started to cross the bridge but underneath the bridge lived a big, bad bully bear. The bear said, "I'll eat you up—you and your sody sallyraytus." And he did. |
| **Storyteller 3:** | The little boy did not return home and Grandma said, "That boy is taking too long!" So she sent the little girl to the store. The little girl bought the sody and sang a song home. |
| **Chorus:** | Sody sallyraytus, lickity-split |
| | Grandma's going to bake some biscuits with it. |
| **Storyteller 4:** | She started to cross the bridge but underneath the bridge lived a big, bad bully bear. The bear said, "I ate the little boy. I'll eat you up too—you and your sody sallyraytus." And he did. |
| **Storyteller 5:** | The little girl did not return home and Grandma said, "That girl is taking too long!" So she sent Grandpa to the store. Grandpa bought the sody and sang a song home. |
| **Chorus:** | Sody sallyraytus, lickity split |
| | Grandma's going to bake some biscuits with it. |

**Storyteller 6:** He started to cross bridge but underneath the bridge lived a big, bad bully bear. The bear said, "I ate the little boy, I ate the little girl and I'll eat you up too. You and your sody sallyraytus." And he did.

**Storyteller 7:** Grandpa did not return home and Grandma said, "That old man is taking too long! I'll fetch it myself." So she went to the store. She bought the sody and sang a song home.

**Chorus:** Sody Sallyraytus, lickity split

Grandma's going to bake some biscuits with it.

**Storyteller 8:** She started to cross the bridge but underneath the bridge there lived a big, bad bully bear. The bear said, "I ate the little boy, I ate the little girl, I ate the old man and I'll eat you up too. You and your sody sallyraytus." And he did.

**Storyteller 9:** Now the pet squirrel was home by himself getting hungrier and hungrier. He went to the store. The storekeeper said the little boy, the little girl, the grandpa, and the grandma had all been there to buy sody sallyraytus. So the squirrel started home.

**Storyteller 10:** He began crossing the bridge but underneath the bridge there lived a big, bad bully bear. The bear said, "I ate the little boy, I ate the little girl, I ate the old man, I ate the old woman and I'll eat you up too!"

**Storyteller 11:** "Oh no you won't!" said the little squirrel and lickity-split, he ran up a nearby tree. The big, bad bully bear began climbing that tree and following the squirrel. He growled, "If you can do it with your little legs, then I can do it with my big legs!"

**Storyteller 12:** But the branch could not bear the big, bad bully bear and it broke. Dooooowwwwn he fell. THUD! Well, that bear fell so hard that out bounced the little boy, the little girl, Grandma and Grandpa. And they each still had their sody sallyraytus. They all sang a song home.

**Chorus:** Sody Sallyraytus, lickity split

Grandma's going to bake some biscuits with it.

**Storyteller 13:** And she did. Squirrel sang happily

**Chorus:** Mmm, mmm, mmm

Yummy in my tummy

The biscuits Grandma made us

From sody sallyraytus.

# Turtle and Beaver's Race

**Storyteller 1:** Long ago, turtle lived in a beautiful pond. She rested in the shade of the surrounding trees and sunned herself on the floating logs. In the winter, Turtle headed down to the bottom of the pond to hibernate in the mud.

**Storyteller 2:** While Turtle slept for the winter, Beaver came by and saw the beautiful pond. Beaver exclaimed, "This pond is perfect. I will make my home here!" He began chewing and chomping on logs, creating a dam and a cozy mound for his house.

**Chorus:** Chew! Chomp! Chew! Chomp! Chew! Chomp! Chomp! Chomp!

**Storyteller 3:** In the spring, Turtle woke up and swam to the surface of the pond. Imagine her surprise when she saw how much things had changed. Her beautiful pond was flooded with water. The trees were drowning and there were no floating logs. She saw Beaver chewing and chomping on some logs.

**Chorus:** Chew! Chomp! Chew! Chomp! Chew! Chomp! Chomp! Chomp!

**Storyteller 4:** Turtle asked, "What are you doing?" Beaver answered, "I am chopping more logs for my beautiful home." Turtle looked around and saw the dam and the mound. She replied, "But I have lived here all my life. This is my home."

**Storyteller 5:** Beaver answered, "Not anymore! It's my pond!" Turtle said, "Well, why don't we share the pond? I am sure we could work this out." But Beaver was stubborn. "No! This pond is mine and if you want it back, you'll have to race for it!"

**Storyteller 6:** Turtle did not want to race but she felt she had no choice. It was decided that they would meet the next day and swim from one end of the pond to the other. The animals gathered in great anticipation of the race between Turtle and Beaver. Some cheered for Turtle. Some cheered for Beaver.

**Chorus:** Go Turtle Go! Go Turtle Go!

Go Beaver Go! Go Beaver Go!

**Storyteller 7:** The race began and Beaver, with his flat tail, swam swiftly. Turtle had a hard time keeping up. The animals cheered them on.

**Chorus:** Go Turtle Go! Go Turtle Go!

Go Beaver Go! Go Beaver Go!

**Storyteller 8:** The race continued. Still Beaver forged again and Turtle trailed behind. Suddenly, Turtle had an idea. She swam as fast as she could and when she was next to Beaver's tail, she chomped down. SNAP! Beaver felt the bite and swung his tail out of the water, sending Turtle flying through the air. The animals cheered.

**Chorus:** Go Turtle Go! Go Turtle Go!

Go Beaver Go! Go Beaver Go!

**Storyteller 9:** Turtle flew across to the end of the pond and won the race. Beaver hung his head low. Turtle said, "Beaver, we could still share the pond." But Beaver was too embarrassed about losing that he left the pond. The next time he found a pond, he made sure he asked if he could share the space.

**Storyteller 10:** Once again, turtle had her beautiful pond back. Turtle rested in the shade of the surrounding trees and sunned herself on the floating logs. Whenever someone needed a place to stay, Turtle offered to share.

# The Snooks Family

Storyteller 1: The Snooks Family lived in a nice upstairs apartment. There was Papa Snooks, Mama Snooks, Brother Snooks, and Sister Snooks. Each night, they would light a candle so they could see in the dark.

Storyteller 2: One night, it was time to go to bed. Mama Snooks couldn't find the candlesnuffer so she asked Papa Snooks to blow out the candle. So Papa Snooks stood in front of the candle.

Chorus: He twisted his mouth and blew to the east (BLOW)

But the candle would not blow out

Storyteller 3: Papa Snooks said, "Mama Snooks, why don't you blow out the candle?" So Mama Snooks stood in front of the candle.

Chorus: She twisted her mouth and blew to the west (BLOW)

But the candle would not blow out

Storyteller 4: Mama Snooks said, "Brother Snooks, why don't you blow out the candle?" So Brother Snooks stood in front of the candle.

Chorus: He twisted his mouth and blew to the north (BLOW)

But the candle would not blow out

Storyteller 5: Brother Snooks said, "Sister Snooks, why don't you blow out the candle? So Sister Snooks stood in front of the candle.

Chorus: She twisted her mouth and blew to the south (BLOW)

But the candle would not blow out

**Storyteller 6:** None of the Snooks family could blow out the candle! Sister Snooks looked out the window and saw a policeman downstairs. She said, "Papa, mama, there is a police man downstairs. Maybe he can help us." So Papa Snooks asked the policeman for help.

**Storyteller 7:** The policeman came upstairs and stood in front of the candle.

**Chorus:** He held his mouth straight and blew straight ahead

And the candle went out! Snuff.

**Storyteller 8:** Mama Snooks said, "Oh no! It's dark in here. We'll never be able to see to walk you out, Mr. Policeman." So she lit the candle.

**Storyteller 9:** Papa Snooks walked the policeman downstairs and waved goodbye. When he returned upstairs, Mama Snooks said, "Papa Snooks, why don't you blow out the candle?"

**Chorus:** Oh no! Here we go again!!!

Enough's snuff!

# American Tall Tales

# Baby Paul Bunyan

Storyteller 1:   If you go to the North Woods of Maine and ask the loggers who the mightiest logger of all is, there is only one answer: Paul Bunyan. He was born a very big baby. His poor mama. Paul Bunyan weighed over 200 pounds at birth!

Chorus:   Bigger than a horse,

Bigger than a cow,

Paul Bunyan was

The biggest baby around.

Storyteller 2:   At three weeks old, Baby Paul Bunyan rolled around in his sleep so much that he knocked down miles and miles of standing timber. People would run in all directions away from the crashing timber. So the government told Baby Paul's parents that they had to take him away.

Chorus:   Bigger than a horse,

Bigger than a cow,

Paul Bunyan was

The biggest baby around.

Storyteller 3:   Baby Paul Bunyan's parents tried to soothe him by placing him in a floating cradle off the coast of Eastport. But Paul was a restless baby and rocked his cradle hard. His rocking created such a swell that the waves crested into tidal surges that crashed down upon all the seaside villages. They say the waves near Nova Scotia were so high that it nearly became an island instead of a peninsula.

**Chorus:**   Bigger than a horse,

Bigger than a cow,

Paul Bunyan was

The biggest baby around.

**Storyteller 4:**   Baby Paul was so big that his mother and father had to have fourteen cows to supply milk for his porridge. Every morning when they looked at him, it seemed that he grew two feet bigger! Finally, his parents decided to move him into the woods where they were sure he would cause no more mischief.

**Storyteller 5:**   When Baby Paul was only seven months old, he climbed out of the huge crib his daddy made for him. He grabbed an axe and started chopping off the legs from his daddy's bed. The bed fell to the ground in a big THUMP and Paul's daddy woke up.

**Storyteller 6:**   Paul's daddy exclaimed, "Honey, wake up!" Paul's mother opened her eyes and was surprised to see Paul waving the axe in one hand and holding a fistful of four by eights in the other. His daddy said, "Why Baby Paul's a born logger for sure! He's got such strength!"

**Chorus:**   Bigger than a horse,

Bigger than a cow,

Paul Bunyan was

The biggest baby around.

**Storyteller 7:**   His mother said proudly, "He's going to be the mightiest logger around!" And you know what? They were right. Paul Bunyan, the world's biggest baby, grew up to be the mightiest logger anyone has ever seen then or now.

**Chorus:**   Bigger than a horse,

Bigger than a cow,

Paul Bunyan was

The biggest baby around.

# Paul Bunyan and the Great Popcorn Blizzard

**Storyteller 1:** Paul Bunyan was the mightiest logger in all of the North Woods. He was a giant man and he was so strong he could take a tree and snap it in half with his bare hands. His animal companion was Babe the Blue Ox and Paul headed a large logging camp.

**Storyteller 2:** After Paul chopped down the trees of North Dakota, he decided that it was time to head west. He and his men loaded their heavy equipment onto a boat that would travel down the Mississippi. It was going to be a long journey across the hot plains.

**Storyteller 3:** Paul and Babe the Blue Ox began leading the way west. Paul said to his men, "You better not get too thirsty because there isn't much water to be had along the hot plains." On and on they trudged but the heat was too much. His men began to tire.

**Chorus:** We're baking in this sizzling heat.

We need to rest our weary feet!

**Storyteller 4:** Hot Biscuit Slim, the camp's cook said, "I made us some vanilla ice cream but it's so hot that the ice cream began to boil!" Paul Bunyan's men said

**Chorus:** We're baking in this sizzling heat.

We need to rest our weary feet!

63

**Storyteller 5:** But on they had to travel across the plains. Even Ole the Big Swede, who was the largest man in camp next to Paul, was growing tired. The men missed the cool shade of the tall trees. Paul Bunyan's men said

**Chorus:** We're baking in this sizzling heat.

We need to rest our weary feet!

**Storyteller 6:** Paul Bunyan himself became so tired that he began dragging his double-bitted axe behind him. The weight of the blade carved a ditch into the ground that became known as the Grand Canyon. Finally, it became so hot that the men refused to go any further. Paul Bunyan's men said

**Chorus:** We're baking in this sizzling heat.

We need to rest our weary feet!

**Storyteller 7:** Hot Slim Biscuit said, "We're running out of food." So Paul went to the mountains. There, he found a farmer who had a barn full of corn. Paul bought the corn and brought it back to the men to feed them. But it was so hot that the corn began popping!

**Chorus:** [bouncing up and down like popcorn]

POP POP POP POP POP

POP POP POP POP POP

**Storyteller 8:** The popcorn fell to the ground like snowflakes. It covered the ground in white and Paul's men thought they were in the middle of a snow blizzard. In fact, they were so cold that they pulled out their coats, mittens and scarves. They had to cover the horses in wool blankets so they would not freeze. They began making snow angels and having popcorn snowball fights. The popcorn snow kept falling.

**Chorus:** [bouncing up and down like popcorn]

POP POP POP POP POP

POP POP POP POP POP

**Storyteller 9:** The men were so happy to escape the heat and they were able to travel again. After traveling through the "snow," they finally reached the great forest in the West. Only Paul and Babe the Blue Ox knew the truth. Whenever anyone would mention the "Great Snow Blizzard," Babe would wink and Paul and Paul would smile back.

**Chorus:** [bouncing up and down like popcorn]

POP POP POP POP POP

POP POP POP POP POP

# Annie Christmas

**Storyteller 1:** As mysterious as New Orleans and as powerful as the Mississippi River she worked on, Annie Christmas was an extraordinary woman. She worked among the toughest men.

**Storyteller 2:** She stood 7 feet tall, maybe higher, and worked her own keelboat. She had 12 sons who were just as big as she was. Her voice was as loud as a foghorn and every stevedore would jump when Annie Christmas snapped her fingers.

**Storyteller 3:** Why, she could carry a barrel of flour under each arm and one on top of her head too! No one dared to cross Annie Christmas because she could lick a dozen men with one hand tied behind her back. "As strong as Annie Christmas" became the saying up and down the river.

**Chorus:** Up the river, down the river, rollin' right along

Annie Christmas was a lady who was tough and strong.

**Storyteller 4:** One day Mike Fink, a newcomer to town, said to Annie Christmas, "The river ain't no place for a lady. You should be at home darning socks out of cotton, not making a fool of yourself hauling cotton bales."

**Storyteller 5:** Annie Christmas was furious. With that, she picked up a bale of cotton with one hand and slammed it into the Mississippi River. The force from the bale was so great that a huge tidal wave rose up and swept Mike Fink away. All the way to Natchez, Mississippi.

**Chorus:** Up the river, down the river, rollin' right along

Annie Christmas was a lady who was tough and strong.

**Storyteller 6:** But Annie Christmas also had a softer side. She liked to get gussied up and prance around town. One day, she had her seamstress make her a fire red gown out of the finest silk from China. It took a whole bolt to sew that dress and it had more gathers than the curtains in the White House.

**Storyteller 7:** When Annie Christmas walked down the street in that gorgeous red gown and her feathered hat, people couldn't help but stare. She had such a royal presence. It was that night that she and Charlie, a riverboat gambler, fell in love.

**Chorus:** Up the river, down the river, rollin' right along

Annie Christmas was a lady who was tough and strong.

**Storyteller 8:** But love had a way of making Annie Christmas soft. All night long, she stayed by Charlie's side and all night long, he kept on winning. "You're my lucky charm," he said to her as she blushed.

**Storyteller 9:** What Annie didn't know was that Charlie was a married man. Their luck would soon run out. Charlene, Charlie's jealous wife, walked onto the boat and saw Annie Christmas with her husband. There, at the hands of Charlie's wife, Annie Christmas met her end.

**Storyteller 10:** In the end, Annie didn't lose her life to the river, she lost her life to love. She was set out in a large coffin on a black barge. Annie Christmas was laid to rest in the place that she loved best—the Mississippi River.

**Chorus:** Up the river, down the river, rollin' right along

Annie Christmas was a lady who was tough and strong.

# Pecos Bill

**Storyteller 1:** Pecos Bill was the greatest cowboy that ever lived. When he was just a baby, his daddy decided that he didn't like being crowded by the neighbors. So he took his 17 children, packed 'em in a wagon and moved out west.

**Storyteller 2:** As Bill's family was crossing the Pecos River, Bill tumbled out. Since then, he has been known as Pecos Bill. His parents didn't discover he was gone until weeks later and by then, they figured it was too late. But Bill was a tough little feller and he was found by a coyote.

**Storyteller 3:** He grew up running with a pack of coyotes. Pecos Bill thought he was a coyote too. One day, a man on a horse came riding by. It was quite a shock for the man to see Pecos Bill because Bill wasn't wearing any clothes. The man asked, "Where are your clothes?"

**Storyteller 4:** Bill answered, "I'm a coyote and coyotes don't wear no clothes." The cowboy said, "No you're not. You're a human." Pecos Bill answered, "But I have fleas and I howl at night. That means I'm a coyote." The cowboy laughed, "Everyone knows that all Texans have fleas and most of 'em howl at night. Coyotes have tails and you don't."

**Storyteller 5:** So the cowboy showed Bill that he had no tail and Pecos Bill realized his true nature. But living with coyotes all those years gave Pecos Bill some pretty special abilities and soon, he became a rootin', tootin' cowboy.

**Chorus:** Pecos Bill was from the Southwest.

There were other cowboys but he was the best.

**Storyteller 6:** When Pecos Bill was brought back to the ranch, the other cowboys made fun of him. They tried to trick Bill but they

67

couldn't outwit him or outsmart him. Pecos Bill asked, "Who's the boss of this outfit?" Gun Smith said, "I was but now you be the boss. You sure are a rootin', tootin' cowboy."

**Chorus:** Pecos Bill was from the Southwest.

There were other cowboys but he was the best.

**Storyteller 7:** So Pecos Bill became the boss cowboy. He invented the lasso by using a 42-foot snake as a rope. Instead of buying a horse from town, Pecos Bill roped himself a wild, bucking bronco. His horse was named Lightning. Pecos Bill was so good at ropin' that he could snare a whole herd of cattle with one lariat. He was a rootin', tootin' cowboy.

**Chorus:** Pecos Bill was from the Southwest.

There were other cowboys but he was the best.

**Storyteller 8:** Some say that Pecos Bill got tired of hauling in water from the Gulf of Mexico so one day, he dug the Grand Canyon. Pecos Bill was never thrown off the back of any animal—a cougar, a bear, or a horse. Why once, he even rode a cyclone bareback.

**Storyteller 9:** Pecos Bill threw his lariat and lassoed the cyclone by the neck. But the cyclone didn't take too kindly to Bill's presence. It lashed and snapped and twirled and whirled. For days, Bill tried to tame that tornado but each was as stubborn as the other. He rode that cyclone over three states until he finally came down in California. That spot where Pecos Bill hog-tied that cyclone is known as Death Valley. He sure was a rootin', tootin' cowboy.

**Chorus:** Pecos Bill was from the Southwest.

There were other cowboys but he was the best.

**Storyteller 10:** When Bill met Slue-Foot Sue, he fell head over spurs in love with her. One day, Slue-Foot Sue insisted on riding Lightning, Bill's horse. Now Lightning didn't let *anyone* ride him except Bill. As soon as she saddled up, Lightning bucked and sent Slue-Foot Sue sailing through the sky. Some say she bounced a few times on account of her hoop skirt but she never came back down.

**Storyteller 11:** How Pecos Bill met his end is still debated to this day. Some say he disappeared, searching for Slue-Foot Sue. Others say he ate some barbed wire and it rusted his insides. Still, others say he laughed himself to death one day. But there's one thing you can't dispute: Pecos Bill sure was a rootin', tootin' cowboy.

**Chorus:** Pecos Bill was from the Southwest.

There were other cowboys but he was the best.

# Source Notes

"Annie Christmas" was adapted from research from The Historic New Orleans Collection, "Strong as Annie Christmas" in *From Sea to Shining Sea*, compiled by Amy L. Cohn (New York, NY: Scholastic Inc., 1993) and "Annie Christmas" in *A Treasury of North American Folktales*, compiled by Catherine Peck (New York, NY: The Philip Lief Group, Inc., 1998).

"Ant and the Grasshopper, The" was adapted from "The Ants and the Grasshopper" in *Aesop's Fables*, selected and adapted by Jack Zipes (New York, NY: The Penguin Group, 1992) and "The Ants and the Grasshopper" in *The Aesop for Children* (New York, NY: Scholastic, Inc., 1994).

"Baby Paul Bunyan" was adapted from "Paul Bunyan and His Boyhood" in *Paul Bunyan Swings His Axe*, by Dell J. McCormick (Caldwell, ID: The Caxton Printers, Ltd., 1962) and "The Birth of Paul Bunyan" in *A Treasury of North American Folktales*, compiled by Catherine Peck (New York, NY: The Philip Lief Group, Inc., 1998).

"Battle of the Firefly and the Apes" was adapted from "Battle of the Firefly and the Apes" in *Book of Fables & Parables*, retold by C.S. Canonigo (Manila, Philippines: CKC Publications, 1996) and "The Firefly and the Apes" in *Near-by Tales*, adapted by Eugene Bahn and Francess Ross (New York, NY: Educational Printing House, Inc., 1939).

"Boy Who Cried Wolf, The" was adapted from childhood memories of "The Boy Who Cried Wolf" told by my parents; "The Shepherd Boy and the Wolf" in *Aesop's Fables*, selected and adapted by Jack Zipes (New York, NY: The Penguin Group, 1992) and "The Shepherd Boy and the Wolf" in *The Aesop for Children* (New York, NY: Scholastic, Inc., 1994).

"Brer Rabbit and the Tar Baby" was adapted from "The Wonderful Tar Baby Story" in *A Treasury of American Folklore*, edited by B.A. Botkin (New York, NY: Crown Publishers, Inc., 1944); "Brer Rabbit and the Tar Baby" in *The Tales of Uncle Remus: The Adventures of Brer Rabbit*, as told by Julius Lester (New York, NY: Dial Books, 1987); and "Brer Fox, Brer Rabbit, and the Tar-Baby" in *The Classic Tales of Brer Rabbit*, retold by David Borgenicht from stories collected by Joel Chandler Harris (Philadelphia, PA: Courage Books, 1995).

"Chicken and the Librarian, The" was adapted from a version passed on me by Hope Baugh, a librarian in Carmel, Indiana in 1998. Thank you, Hope. Upon doing extensive research, I have seen it all over the Internet as a joke or short story with no source attribution.

"Country Mouse and City Mouse, The" was adapted from "The Country Mouse and the Town Mouse" in *Aesop's Fables*, selected and adapted by Jack Zipes (New York, NY: The Penguin Group, 1992) and "The Town Mouse and the Country Mouse" in *The Aesop for Children* (New York, NY: Scholastic, Inc., 1994).

"Epaminondas" was adapted from a version I heard from Dolores Henderson, a storyteller and retired school librarian from Morgan City, Louisiana. Ms. Dolores grew up hearing Epaminondas from her family. I also found a web version on the Internet of "Epaminondas and His Auntie" by Sara Cone Bryant at www.sterlingtimes.org/epaminondas.htm. I have edited the story to reflect a gentler ending but chose to keep the vernacular "ain't got" in the story to preserve the story's cultural flavor.

"Frog and the Ox, The" was adapted from "The Frog and the Ox" in *Aesop's Fables*, selected and adapted by Jack Zipes (New York, NY: The Penguin Group, 1992) and "The Frogs and the Ox" in *The Aesop for Children* (New York, NY: Scholastic, Inc., 1994).

"Gunny Wolf, The" was adapted from "The Gunny Wolf" in *A Treasury of American Folklore*, edited by B.A. Botkin (New York, NY: Crown Publishers, Inc., 1944) and *The Gunniwolf*, retold by Wilhelmina Harper (New York, NY: Dutton Children's Books, 2003; original text, 1918 by Wilhelmina Harper).

"Jack Seeks His Fortune" was adapted from "How Jack Went to Seek His Fortune" in *Troll Treasury of Animal Stories*, edited by John C. Miles (Mahwah, NJ: Harper Collins, 1991) and "Jack and the Robbers" in *The Jack Tales*, by Ray Hicks (New York, NY: Callaway, 2000).

"Lion and the Mouse, The" was adapted from childhood memories of the story; "The Lion and the Mouse" in *Aesop's Fables*, selected and adapted by Jack Zipes (New York, NY: The Penguin Group, 1992) and "The Lion and the Mouse" in *The Aesop for Children* (New York, NY: Scholastic, Inc., 1994).

"Little Red Hen, The" was adapted from childhood memories of the story; "The Little Red Hen and the Grain of Wheat" in *Story Time of My Bookhouse*, edited by Olive Beaupré Miller (Lake Bluff, IL: The Book House for Children, 1965) and "Little Red Hen and the Grains of Wheat" in *Troll Treasury of Animal Stories*, edited by John C. Miles (Mahwah, NJ: Harper Collins, 1991).

"Paul Bunyan and the Great Popcorn Blizzard" was adapted from "The Popcorn Blizzard" in *Paul Bunyan Swings His Axe*, by Dell J. McCormick (Caldwell, ID: The Caxton Printers, Ltd., 1962) and "Paul's Popcorn" in *A Treasury of North American Folktales*, compiled by Catherine Peck (New York, NY: The Philip Lief Group, Inc., 1998).

"Pecos Bill" was adapted from *Pecos Bill*, by Nanci A. Lyman (Mahwah, NJ: Troll Associates, 1980); "The Saga of Pecos Bill" in *A Treasury of American Folklore*, edited by B.A. Botkin (New York, NY: Crown Publishers, Inc., 1944); and "Ride 'em, Round 'em, Rope 'em: The Story of Pecos Bill," retold by Brian Gleeson in *From Sea to Shining Sea*, compiled by Amy L. Cohn (New York, NY: Scholastic Inc., 1993).

"Sausage Nose" was adapted from "The Sausage" in *Folkfest: Folktales from Around the World*, by Doug Sylvester (San Diego, CA: Rainbow Horizons Publishing, 1987) and "The Sausage" in *Fairy Tales from the Swedish*, by Gabriel Djurklou, translated by H. L. Brækstad (Philadelphia and New York: J. B. Lippincott Company, 1901).

"Snooks Family, The" was adapted from a version told to me by my friend Gale Criswell, children's librarian and Youth Services Consultant for the State Library of Louisiana and "The Twist-Mouth Family" in *From Sea to Shining Sea*, compiled by Amy L. Cohn (New York, NY: Scholastic Inc., 1993).

"Sody Sallyraytus" was adapted from "Sody Sallyraytus" in *Grandfather Tales*, collected and retold by Richard Chase (Cambridge, MA: The Riverside Press, 1948) and "Sody Saleratus" in *Crocodile! Crocodile! Stories Told Around the World*, by Barbara Baumgartner (New York, NY: Dorling Kindersley Publishing, Inc., 1994).

"Tortoise and the Hare, The" was adapted from childhood memories of the story; "The Hare and the Tortoise" in *Aesop's Fables*, selected and adapted by Jack Zipes (New York, NY: The

Penguin Group, 1992) and "The Tortoise and the Hare" in *Troll Treasury of Animal Stories*, edited by John C. Miles (Mahwah, NJ: Harper Collins, 1991).

"Turtle and Beaver's Race" was adapted from *Turtle's Race with Beaver*, as told by Joseph Bruchac and James Bruchac (New York, NY: Dial Books for Young Readers, 2003) and "Turtle Races with Beaver" in the *Puddler Activity Guide* www.greenwing.org/teachersguide/win02/win02moreabt.htm.

"Turtle Who Could Not Stop Talking, The" was adapted from "The Talkative Tortoise" in *Indian Fairy Tales*, collected by Joseph Jacobs (New York, NY: Dover Publications, 1969; originally published in 1892).

"The Ugly Duckling" was adapted from childhood memories of the story and "The Ugly Little Duck" in *Anderson's Fairy Tales*, by Hans Christian Anderson (New York, NY: Anness Publishing Limited, 1995).

"Wee, Wee Mannie and the Big, Big Coo, The" was adapted from "The Wee, Wee Mannie and the Big, Big Coo" in *Up One Pair of Stairs of My Book House*, edited by Olive Beaupré Miller (Lake Bluff, IL: The Book House for Children, 1965); "The Wee, Wee Mannie and the Big, Big Coo" in *Folkfest: Folktales from Around the World*, by Doug Sylvester (San Diego, CA: Rainbow Horizons Publishing, 1987).

"Why the Bear is Stumpy-Tailed" was adapted from "Why the Bear is Stumpy-Tailed" in *The Arbuthnot Anthology of Children's Literature Third Edition*, edited by Mark Taylor (Glenview, IL: Scott, Foresman and Company, 1970), and "Why the Bear is Stumpy-Tailed" in *Troll Treasury of Animal Stories*, edited by John C. Miles (Mahwah, NJ: Harper Collins, 1991).

# Resources

Below are some print and web resources that will help you in creating your own story theater scripts and working with student storytellers.

# Bibliography

Collins, Rives and Cooper, Pamela; *The Power of Story – Teaching Through Storytelling*; Gorsuch Scarisbrick Publishers (1997).

Gillard, Marni; *Story Teller Story Teacher*; Stenhouse Publishers (1996).

Griffin, Barbara Budge; *Students as Storytellers The Long and Short of Learning a Story*; Griffin McKay Publications (1995).

Kinghorn, Harriet R. and Pelton, Mary Helen; *Every Child a Storyteller – A Handbook of Ideas*; Teacher Ideas Press (1991).

National Storytelling Network, *Tales as Tools*; The National Storytelling Press (1994).

Sima, Judy and Cordi, Kevin, *Raising Voices: Youth Storytelling Groups and Troupes*; Libraries Unlimited (2003).

# Webliography

The Internet is a great place for story research. Here are some of my favorite story sites.

American Folktales: www.americanfolklore.net. This site has at least one folktale from every state.

Ashliman's Folktales and Fairytales: www.pitt.edu/~dash/ashliman.html. Professor D.L. Ashliman, through the University of Pittsburgh, maintains one of the best comprehensive websites on folk and fairy tales.

Absolutely Whootie Stories to Grow By: www.storiestogrowby.com. A fabulous site with folk and fairy tales from around the world developed especially for kids. Teachers will enjoy the lesson plans and educational content of the site.

Chris King's Storytelling Power: www.creativekeys.net/StorytellingPower/sphome.html. Chris King provides a great site on the how-to of storytelling. It's chock full of ideas and articles on the power of storytelling. In addition, her site highlights the best in storytelling resource books.

Heather Forest's StoryArts: www.storyarts.org. Storyteller Heather Forest offers lesson plans and activities, articles, and a curriculum ideas exchange.

Scholastic's Myths, Folktales & Fairy Tales: http://teacher.scholastic.com/writewit/mff/. Explore stories from around the world, discover folktale writing, take a storytelling workshop and meet authors.

The Story Connection: www.storyconnection.net. This my site, which has a section for teachers (The Classroom Connection) and a Storytelling Activities section with over 15 activities to do with kids.

Turner South Learning Through Storytelling: www.turnerlearning.com/turnersouth/ storytelling/. On this site, you can take an online workshop on teaching kids to tell stories. In addition, the site lists extension activities and resources.

# Index of Stories